This Book Belongs To

....

Author & Digital Artist
Pam Henderson

My First Pony Club

This is a story of a very shy pony named Barnaby.

Barnaby loved his paddock. It was quiet, it smelled like sweet grass, and his best friend was a sheep named Shaun. Shaun was always there to nibble clover with him. Barnaby felt safe.

But today was a big day.

"The Pink Pony Cowgirls are going to be at Pony Club today Barnaby, and we have been invited!", his owner, a kind girl named Leonara said to him all excited, as she washed him, then brushed his mane until it shone. Shaun watched on in amazement.

Barnaby's tummy felt like it had
a hundred little butterflies fluttering
around inside. Pony Club?
That sounded loud, that sounded like
a lot of strangers, Barnaby was scared.

He just wanted to stay home with Shaun, where he was safe in his paddock and they could run around and play all day. Leonara saddled up Barnaby. "You will be OK", said Shaun.

Leonara gently climbed onto Barnaby's back and led him out the gate and down the road. It wasn't far to the showgrounds where it was being held.

When they got to the showgrounds, Barnaby stopped short and his eyes went wide with amazement.

There were so many ponies! Ponies of every colour: black ponies, white ponies, grey ponies, brown ponies. Barnaby had never seen so many ponies in his entire life.

It was so loud! The air was full of happy noises: Lots of Neighs! and Snorts! from the horses and giggles from all the children.

Barnaby felt his ears flatten a little, he felt scared, he wanted to hide behind Leonara.

"It's okay buddy," Leonara whispered, giving his neck a gentle pat. "Let's just stand over here and watch for awhile".

They stood near a tall fence with lots of flowers. Barnaby kept his head low.

Suddenly, a small pony with a messy white mane and big friendly brown eyes walked right up to Barnaby and said "Hi!, my name is Pip and this is my owner Scarlett, are you new here?".

Barnaby looked up at Leonara, then back at Pip. Pip wasn't loud or scary. Pip just looked bouncy and happy like himself. Barnaby took a deep breath. "H-hello", he mumbled, I'm Barnaby.

"Welcome to Pony Club Barnaby!" Pip said shaking his messy white mane. "It's so much fun! The Pink Pony Cowgirls are here today doing some

demonstrations, then we all get to have some practice, do you want to go and watch?" "Yes please", said Barnaby. So Barnaby and Pip went off to watch the Cowgirls do their thing.

Barnaby and Pip sat and watched
the Pink Pony Cowgirls do all the tricks
that Barnaby only ever dreamed of doing.

He had so much fun with Pip. It was the best day that Barnaby had ever had.
Now it was Barnaby's time to try some of the tricks. He was very nervous.

They did Barrel Racing.

They tried jumping
different obsticles.

Look no hands! said
Leonara and Scarlett.

Barnaby's tummy didn't feel like it had one hundred butterflies anymore, now it felt like it had one big warm happy sun glowing inside. He had finally made friends.

It was now time for lunch. Everyone gathered together and had a BBQ, while we were given some yummy apples to eat.

It was the best day ever, Barnaby couldn't wait to go home and tell Shaun all about his day and his new friends.

After lunch we all said our goodbyes. "Thank you Pip for showing me the best day of my life, I hope to see you again real soon".

"Of course you will", said Pip,
"I am sure you will be coming
every month from now on".
"I hope so", said Barnaby.

"Hi Shaun, I'm back and I have had the best day. I have so much to tell you, about what I did, and what I have seen, and the friends I have made", said Barnaby all excited.

"Oh Shaun, this was the best day I have ever had. There were lots of people but they were all so nice and friendly and we played lots of games and had a delicious lunch. I wish you could of come". said Barnaby.

It was getting dark, so Barnaby and Shaun got ready for bed.

They both lay down together and drifted off to sleep. Barnaby dreaming of the amazing day he just had.

My First Pony Club

ISBN - 978-0-6457735-2-1